# Blue Etiquette

## Also by Kathleen Driskell

*Laughing Sickness*

*Seed Across Snow*

*Peck and Pock: A Graphic Poem*

*Next Door to the Dead*

# Blue Etiquette

*poems by*

## Kathleen Driskell

 Red Hen Press | *Pasadena, CA*

Book design & layout by Pricilla Delatorre

Library of Congress Cataloging-in-Publication Data

Names: Driskell, Kathleen Mason, author.
Title: Blue etiquette : poems / by Kathleen Driskell.
Description: First edition. | Pasadena, CA : Red Hen Press, [2016]
Identifiers: LCCN 2016023201 (print) | LCCN 2016029864 (ebook) | ISBN
    9781597092388 (softcover : acid-free paper) | ISBN 9781597095150 (ebook)
Classification: LCC PS3604.R56583 A6 2016 (print) | LCC PS3604.R56583 (ebook)
    | DDC 811/.6—dc23
LC record available at https://lccn.loc.gov/2016023201

The National Endowment for the Arts, the Los Angeles County Arts Commission, the
Los Angeles Department of Cultural Affairs, the Dwight Stuart Youth Fund, the Pasadena
Arts & Culture Commission and the City of Pasadena Cultural Affairs Division, the Ah-
manson Foundation, and Sony Pictures Entertainment partially support Red Hen Press.

First Edition
Published by Red Hen Press
www.redhen.org

# Acknowledgments & Thank You Notes

I thank the editors of the following literary magazines for publishing these poems, sometimes in earlier forms: *Appalachian Heritage*: "Laundry Woman," "What I Learned in My Mother's Kitchen," and "Evolution"; *The Cortland Review*: "Cupid"; *The Florida Review*: "Oyster Fork" and "The Fruit Knife" under the titles "Oyster Fork Ode" and "Elegy with Fruit Knife"; *Poems & Plays*: "The Oak Room," and "Church of the Absent Mother"; *Plume*: "Her Mother's Marriages Drift like Boats"; *Rattle*: "In a Diner Somewhere in Iowa, I Imagine My Father Meeting the Future President"; *Shenandoah*: "What the Girl Wore," later featured on Poetry Daily; and *Still: The Journal*: "Young Angel of Darkness," "At New Hope Facility," "Water Baby," and "On Cleaving."

As always, I am grateful to my colleagues at Spalding University's low-residency MFA in Writing Program for their friendship and professional insights. I also wish to express gratitude to my talented poet and writer friends Gaylord Brewer, Sherry Chandler, Jim Clark, Adam Day, Lynnell Edwards, Lauren Harr, Silas House, Jason Howard, Erin Keane, Terry Kennedy, Ellyn Lichvar, Caitlin McCann, Katerina Stoykova-Klemer, Marianne Worthington, and Julie Wrinn for offering ongoing encouragement and support. And I have deep appreciation for all who work so tirelessly for writers at The Carnegie Center for Literacy and Learning in Lexington, Kentucky.

And finally my greatest appreciation goes to my husband, Terry, and my children, Wyatt and Quinn. You fill my life with laughter, delight, and love.

*In Memory*

*Claudia Emerson*

*1957–2014*

# Contents

## American Anthem

# The Best People

# Advice to the Novice

## In a Time of Bereavement

# Blue Etiquette

# American Anthem

*We must stand whenever it is played or sung to us; this means in our presence. We do not rise, however, when it accompanies the action seen on the stage or the screen—because we have no part in the scene.*

—E.P.

## Mowing the Fairways

One summer, at the local course,
I spent my hot days driving the beat-up
Allis-Chalmers, black smoke burping

from its stack. Up and down
the fairways of the back nine
I rumbled, bush-hogging the rough.

I stopped looking behind me
after the first day, when I realized
I was mowing over nests of young.

Once, a shredded snake flew
overhead, strange tentacled bird, thrown
up from the churning rusted blades.

It was how I was going to escape, to get myself
to college, after the sheriff had run away
my father. How I would become a nurse,

or a teacher, or a paralegal. Something
useful.

   I didn't have to begin ducking balls
until around lunch, when the duffers,

who'd told lies to escape their offices
for the afternoon, sped about in carts
for a quick round. Once, cutting

farthest from the clubhouse,
I watched three men
in bright orange jumpsuits

navigate the wood's edge. They saw
that I saw them, but we all pretended
I hadn't. They kept moving.

I kept mowing. Trundling forward,
we were all—I guess—pretending it
didn't matter where we'd just come from.

## What I Learned in My Mother's Kitchen

While my father traveled for his job during the week,
my mother lived the life of a woman emancipated
by TV dinners and pizza delivery. On Sundays, though,
after church, my father dragged her back to the kitchen,
where she worked the opener against the lip of a can
of salmon so awkwardly I stuck around to make sure
that when she fished out the snaggletoothed lid,
she didn't cut herself and need some stitches. While her
cigarette smoldered in the pink melamine ashtray,
she sputtered, crushing the tiles of saltines with her
manicured hands, plunging ten fingers, tips painted bright
pink, into the bowl of heaped cracker dust and gray skin.
I watched her jaw tighten when through her powerful fists,
she squeezed and crunched the fragile feathery bone.

## At New Hope Facility

Each night I brushed
their ragged teeth, delicate and
sharp as those
in a baby's mouth and I lifted
them into bed,
and tucked blankets up under them,
their curled runt hands
set at their chests like the useless
claws of dinosaurs.
I walked and walked, back and forth,
the entire shift,
answering their soft bells, pretending
I could take care of each of them,
though truly I was in sore want
of my own mother. I was
out to prove I needed no one,
nor any of their money if that meant
bending even a tiny bit
to their wills. I felt leashed to that
place as if a beast,
wretched and filled with abundant
and fulsome, fulsome
sorrow. Every night I walked down
the long pod, I grimaced
at the noise my sneakers made, worried

that each loud squeak would wake
all those I had just lashed to bed.
I imagined my shoe-squeaks
calling to them like the sweet sirens
of autonomy,
which I knew I had, and knowing
that, somehow, made
me feel at least a little better.

## Water Baby

That year I was trying to escape it all
in New Hope, a bleak place
where I'd wheel the residents
back and forth to their meals

and therapy. I had convinced myself
I was doing good, but was so awkward
and ill at ease among them.
I was a young woman

who could walk and talk and
return to college any time
she damn well got her act together
and I knew it. And they knew it too—

all the teen-aged girls I lifted about
like wet cardboard boxes.
When the nurse's aide first walked me
through the halls, and called them *water babies*

I'd imagined something fluid
and beautifully alien as a jellyfish,
but Christine's water baby head
was so enormously heavy she listed perpetually

to the left. She was a twisted burl
of a girl. We took an instant dislike
to each other. She fought me
all the way—cursing

as I pushed her to the shower,
undressed her, tried to soap her
down, finding it nearly impossible
to lift her frozen limbs

out of their unreasonable creases.
One evening, blood splattered beneath
her chair, great red splotches of it
against the white tile

of the community shower.
Near my shoe, a tight splat dropped
and bloomed like a peony unfisting
in a field of snow. It gave me pause, but

then I hosed her blood down the drain
while she slumped behind me
in her shower chair: her hair,
thin, knotted, dripping,

her feral anger rising
with the steam.
Whatever.
I knew I would always win
simply by punching out,

walking free from the frozen fields
surrounding that institutionalized place.
At twenty, that's what I knew
of leaving, never once believing

I'd ever think of her again, never
bothering to look down to see
the blood spattered across the toes of
my white sneakers, little seeds taking root.

## American Bison

The operator thinks I'm nuts when I call 911
to report them grazing in my suburban backyard;

she's musing about which agency to dial,
I hear her flipping pages, say she

has to check with her supervisor, say
she'll phone me back in a few. I just wish

they'd waft away, but the He-Bison, taller
than my old Volvo, looks as if he's not

going anywhere; he's shaggy and obtuse,
a dull fellow methodically chewing

a sprig torn from my azalea bush, my blossoms
grinding into a foamy pink slather

between his teeth, enormous, flat, yellow. If I had
a good arm, I could toss a ring and hoop his horn

from my window, but he doesn't even turn to look
when I crank it open and yell *Shoo! Yoo-hoo!*

*Buffalo! Shoo!* He's oblivious. He's king after all,
but my shouting has given the poor she-bison a start.

Nervous Nelly. She jumps to the side, in three dainty
hops; when she stops, she turns rigid as the already-

taxidermied, perfectly poised, as if on display
upon my clipped lawn. She only needs a price tag

pinned to her silly little ear. Her only movement,
panic nickering around the edge of her eyes.

Her shoulders lose tension. Her face slackens.
Her nubby horns droop. It's as if just then she's realized—

and in that instant regretted—how placidly she followed him
through the farmer's jolly green field, and through

the broken fence. Big dumb bull, his eyes drugged
with chewing pleasure. Her face now seems

filled with disgust and I wonder if she sees what I see:
from his wet sloppy snout, great strands of snot blow

loopily through the spring breeze like a wild trapeze.
I find myself then thinking of my former student, the one

found dead, strangled by her boyfriend. How on TV
he looked so stupid, so incapable of anything big,

yet, she'd loved him she'd written in a paper
handed in to me. She wore her hair parted on the side

so that it hid what was often her bruised eye.
I saw it more than once, considered how

he must have been left-handed for she was
always bruised on the right side. She wanted

to be a writer. I remember thinking she had things
to write about. And there were other girls, women,

other calls to 911. And I came that close, and not
just once—ah, the she-bison, still in my yard

seems quieter now, almost resigned, too. Her dumb
fellow is blank-eyed, entranced with the music

of his cud being chewed in his own head, but
she and I seem to be listening for

the truck, the warden, the gun, the whizzling
quick whistle of the anesthetizing dart.

*On Cleaving*

All summer I watched for him. I knew he was out there,
inside the rimming of woods that ran all around.

Wild boy, his feral curls stiff and ashy with dirt,
he pedaled past at least once a day on his rickety rusting

bicycle, grocery bags dangling from crooked handlebars,
his filthy sleeping bag tied to the rear fender. One

neighbor said she saw him washing dishes at the Waffle House,
near the exit ramp. Another called the cops, but no one ever

found out what he was hiding from or why. Though I tried
to stay alert, he always approached quietly, giving me a start

while out front pulling weeds near the picket gate. Each time
he appeared, my heart revved up in faster time, my eyes anxiously

searching for my small children nearby, digging happily
in the dirt with old spoons. All summer, he must have lain

in the woods, awkwardly tending his fugitive camp, trying
to slow his own heart leaping up with each odd bird call

or snap. In the night, I'd wander from window
to window, watching, making sure his flame

had not caught hold of the horizon. I buttressed for
danger, instead of worrying over him like a good mother,

instead of extending him any kindness, if only
in my mind. So many ways my children have cleaved

my heart tenderly toward the world; and so many ways
they've turned my grizzly core against it.

## Evolution

Aspiring to college,
I set out
to evolve more quickly
than the finches
and tortoises
I'd read about, and more
quickly than the coal miners
and factory workers
I'd come from and
after just one summer
in loose brown polyester,
and awful white shoes,
the required waitress uniform
at the country club,
where I set limp Dover sole
in front of lunching ladies
I moved into the hot tuxedo
I wore at a five-star, where tableside
I often cracked a coddled egg
and divided the bulb of yolk yellow
from the sticky white viscosity
and addressed the anchovy,
until its hairy bones were mashed,
and then the lemon squeeze,
and the Tabasco, eight quick drops.
Sitting next to the older men
in expensive suits and shoes,
young beautiful women
in narrow sequined dresses

tried to ignore me as I tossed
their garlicky salad,
and deftly used my Russian
service. With each of them,
I was just as haughty, plating
their leafy vinegary greens
with disdain, because like Darwin,
I hadn't seen, at first, that these
women were also determined to evolve.

## Grand Opening: The Seelbach Hotel, Louisville

When I worked at the four-star restaurant
within the great hotel recently bought and
emptied of syringes and beer bottles by the B-actor,

I learned all about cutlery, learned there
was such a thing as a sardine fork, and how
pretty it truly was, perhaps because of its limited use.

I learned the bon-bon spoon, and the difference
between high and low tea and how to arrange pretty
pink frosted nibbles on a chilled scalloped plate.

I was given a taste of *foie gras*, so I would know
how to describe the expensive texture to our guests,
and I learned the difference between the regions

and great grapes, from Graves to Grenache, and how
to properly pronounce claret. I memorized
the five mother sauces and recited them back

to Jean-Pierre, the maître d', who assured this
was the only way I could rise in the world.
I learned how to stay out of the kitchen

when the chef brandished his big knife,
surprised, that despite his training at the CIA,
he was nothing but cliché. I learned

how to hold in a snigger while hurrying
back to the kitchen, when a couple, *amateurs,*
we called them, ill-dressed and ill-at-ease, had to be led

through their anniversary dinner by waiters.
In the dining room, we were easy-going, patient
with them, but annoyed, too. How could we not be

when they hadn't the sense to enjoy their *chateaubriand,*
as we would have, had the hotel management not
barred us from eating there on our nights off.

## The Oak Room

I had to stand tip-toed to hold my edge
of the tablecloth high enough, while

my captain held the other side—teams
of waiters circled Table 16 in this way—

as if we were keeping private a young lady
emerging from her soapy bath. But inside

our ring of sheets, a fat man lay on the floor
while my maître d' performed a rough CPR—

clothes twisted, shirt nearly off, the man's red
belly shook with each artificial compression.

I saw on his table, a carafe Jean-Pierre
had just decanted, a rack of lamb,

served minutes before from the left by Lenny—
three ribs chewed clean and in a pile

to the side of his plate. Two chops remained
for LeSean to clear from the table.

My eyes then fixed on a crust of bread
fallen to the burgundy carpet. Outside

the circle, six or eight tables remained
and somehow our co-workers were managing

to continue dinner service; the dining room
was full of couples on dates or celebrating

anniversaries, unwilling to leave the food
they'd been waiting months to enjoy.

The guests chewed on and on, trying
to pretend this meat was forgettable.

Sirens sounded in the street
under the arched windows. The EMTs

rumbled, rushing up the winding staircase.
And, then, people gasped. Red light

swirled around the walls of the dining
room. Mohammad, the handsome head waiter,

had just put a match to a brandied pan
of bubbling cherries jubilee.

## American Blason

My own eyes are not a thing like the sun's,
but like Shakespeare's muse my breasts are kind of
dun and so are my feet, now that I look more
closely. Older now, thin-skinned and bony,
blue veins ridge along them as if my worn feet
are a topographical map in high relief, the map
of a country so poor, so rugged and remote
no tourist would ever consider traveling there.

And, yet, it occurs to me now, that I love these
tired old feet, remembering all those places
they have lifted and set me down to, even
those rough cowboy bars, the tawdry bus stations
at 2:00 a.m., the bright Waffle House off Route 1A,
the small cell where one night I was locked up
with three middle-aged prostitutes who took me
under the gentle wings of their fake fur coats
and synthetic wigs which hung down in tight braids

and agreed with all their street smarts that, *no
baby*, I didn't belong locked up there
with them. Those prostitutes were like Shakespeare
in that they saw me clearly, simplified
in front of them, but unlike Shakespeare, they
told me lies and I was happy that grim morning,
just before I made bail, to believe them, for back then,
I was only able to love the person I was not to be.

*Have Silver That Shines or None*


On Derby night, we finally set the entrees
on Table 42, and 8 of us, in our streaked
white tuxedos, stood around the round-top
and 1-2-3 lifted the silver globes off
each plate with 1 flourish. The host looked down
at his plate, the charred nub of a fillet, then
chucked it at me. The entire plate of food.
A glob of Bordelaise stuck 2 my cheek.
His horse hadn't placed 1, 2, or 3,
Table 42 had been waiting over 1 hour 4
supper, & his supper was not 2 his liking.

## Old Maître D'

He can hardly believe it
has come to this, minding
Mrs. Worldly and the other
old-money women who order
veal scaloppini and arugula
with hearts of palm and push it
around their plates until
the Manhattans made with
their husbands' best bourbon
are set shimmering at the table.

Good god, they can drink.
If the waiter brings the check
too quickly, tries to herd them
out to their drivers too quickly,
the hags will have his head.
But if he waits too long,
their husbands will have his job.

He used to wear a couture tuxedo
just inside the door of the finest
four-star restaurant in town,
where his clients were eager
to know what he thought of
the newest grape (it won't lay
well, best to drink it now . . .
*if at all, he-he*), or fusion foods

(my lord, *really*, pheasant
impaled on flaming bamboo?)
but he's fallen, how he's
fallen here to near ashes.

## Café Diablo

*A Recipe Remembered*

My job is to watch
              but not learn,
   hand, but not
        handle,
  to carry,
        but not carry on,
so when his pink
  soft palm
comes out,
   I place the match there
   (alongside its neat box).

        The sound of the match striking
   is the sound of a zipper unzipping
and awhoosh,
        the gleaming copper réchaud quickens in the dark.

   The captain's hand shakes the match quiet
the way a nurse shakes a thermometer:
        I hold out my palm

     which seems yellow and hard compared to his
       and he tosses the charred twist there
     as if I'm an ashtray.

I ignore the echo of the stigmata. I know

enough to know

this check is going to be expensive
        and I want my cut.

    Around the table, across the white linen,
        the businessmen lean, tilt and talk, making deals
                with each other, while their young women—
                    the redhead
has her finger against her wet bottom lip,
            the brunette's eyes are full and pooling—
watch my captain, beautiful captain!

                waggle his sharp knife against the orange rind,
                    the peel peeling off as if in slow striptease,

    dropping seductively into a coil.

        My turn to stud
                the spring of rind with the hard pointed tacks
of cloves. Each clove prick chucks
            into the air a titillating mist of orange scent.

    Captain closes his eyes,
            leans into the smell
    and sniffs twice,
                then looks directly at the redhead
                and smiles without showing his teeth. He's working

his knife against the yellow thick skin
of a plump lemon,
and when finished, hands the skin to me.
He watches as I secure the tips of the coiled orange
and lemon into the teeth
of a large silver fork.

If the fragile skins break, I go home
broke . . .

but I manage
and hand it all over.
I smile,
but the captain has no time for me
as he plants his feet,
then raises the fork like a god;
he nods.
I pour slippery Gran Marnier into the empty ladle
in his other hand. First, the ladle passes

over the fire. My captain pretends to be shy,

though back in the kitchen, when he yells
at the sous chef, foam forms
in the corners of his mouth,
and when spit flies
I act like I haven't felt a thing.
Soon, flame catches the liquor.

He's a lion-tamer now, showing off
                with the burning ladle, its mane, waving it
                higher and
        higher until it's the level of


                the captain's dark eyes, dark lashes,
                        then, he pours the heavy-legged
                orange brandy,
                        tripping aflame down
                the twisted spine of the rinds.

It crackles and snaps,
        clucks like a chicken,
        sparks as the flame licks
                        and singes the cloves. From above


                a pinch of cinnamon is dropped
        and its specks twinkle loudly,
                shower, fall flickering.


                I may be burned,
                        but I may not catch fire.


Watch my captain, handsome
                in his trim tuxedo, dramatic, lit
        by firelight. He pours
                the black strong syrup
        into small porcelain cups.

The Devil says drink this,
   and you'll be good enough to eat,

but not a drop of it
  is meant for me.

# The Best People

*"Mrs. Distinguished, may I present Mr. Traveler?"*
*"Mrs. Young, may I present Professor Gray?"*

—E.P.

## Laundry Woman

My great-grandmother agitated
Mrs. Worldly's wash every week
over the hot flash and glow
of the fire in the misery shed.
Hand on rough stick, grandmother
pulled around the glob
of tangled shirts and sheets;
she stirred as if hauling the weighted
laundry about an axis, sloshy seas
yielding a watery soup, thin gruel, sure,
but nutrition enough to feed her
fatherless children, nutrition enough
to bring us into this unimagined World.

*Interviewing the Applicant*


Mrs. Worldly searched
through references
provided by the Gildings,
the Oldlineages,
and the Wellborns,
checking off the list
of attributes necessary
for the one whom
she'd take into service
as her between maid:
sobriety, capability, piety,
worthiness, trust. Then,
Mrs. made a circular motion
with her wrist, her narrow
pointed finger. I slowly
turned around as she
looked me up and down.
She said she supposed
she liked the look
of me, well enough,
said that I was *hired*.
It's interesting how
in the flushed ear
the sound of that word
throws its snug net out
into the blue pond,
and drags back
its wriggling rhyme,
its sister-word *fired*.

## Billy Blueblood

Just before closing, 2:00 a.m., Billy pulled his Ambassador
into the corrugated lot of the Elkhorn Mountain Tavern,
where my grandmother was bar maid. Billy motioned
for a shot glass and nodded for her to pour. *Come closer,*
he told her, dark-haired, light-eyed, slim despite
the five kids tucked in thin beds at home under the care
of the eleven-year-old. Billy spun a nickel down the bar
and told Randy, the owner, *play something so we can dance*

*slow.* Years later, when I waited tables to get through
college, I was given a card with the name Blueblood,
passed to me by a soft manicured hand. The tip? Less than
15%. No surprise there, really, but stingier still was
the history that had come back to try to claim me.

## The Useful Man

Uncle Buss busied himself
at the Worldlys' Farm:
tinkering the Cook's kettle,
mending rotten pasture
fences, helping Billy
Blueblood out
of his clothes after
 a night on the town,
and, then, the next day,
visiting town to call
upon the mechanic,
to pay him
a very generous sum
to come to the old place
to fix the fender,
to remove dirt
and blood, bits
of fur and muscle
from the grill.

## Justice Putinpowerbycoal

Here's the real story: his deputy drove him out
deep into the hilly poor country and pulled in,
patrolcar puttering at the foot of the rutted drive
below the rough log house of my grandfather,
who'd just blown off the leg of his new young wife.
Justice slowly climbed the hill to the cabin steps,
looked to where on the porch Grandad sat, shotgun
between his legs, his chin resting on the barrel.
*I been waiting for you,* said Granddad. *I figured
you'd want to see this finished.* Justice said,
*I ain't ever wanted to come, to mess in any of you people's
troubles, but I guess best to hand that over.* Granddad
shook his head. *Naw, don't think I will,* he said, and . . .

## Snakepreacher

Old Parson stood under October's
hunter moon, his boots soaked
from the long journey across the wet
clipped grass of Medalbourbon Manor
and he held the slithering serpent high.
Within the round lunar tableau,
from his fist, it writhered and lashed,
spasmed and flicked. Old Mrs. looked
down from her bedroom window,
listened to the preacher recite the Lord's
Prayer a dozen times until she'd had enough.
Old Mr. was supposed to be in Chicago
(again) and so she rang the Useful Man,
handed over her own pistol. Do I even need
to finish telling this story? After all,
he was the Useful Man and had never
seen any want to shoot a rat snake.

## Slow Jiggy

The young heir pulled into the pumps
and laid on his horn. Slow Jiggy came
out to fill the boy up and Hartford
watched small-eyed to make sure Jiggy
squeegeed off every miserable yellow
splat, satisfied only when out came
the clean shammy cloth to shine the glass
up good. Young heir didn't have to tell
Jig to do this. Jiggy was simple, sure,
but he was from Coal County. Born there,
lived there long enough to know who's
who and that even though the mayflies
he cleaned off the window that afternoon
were the last of the season, next spring
he'd be wiping clean their antediluvian kin.
But, he also remembered hearing the old
boys greasing cars up on the racks
in the garage tell about the year the mayflies
swarmed so thick above Cumberland River
they was like fog and caused an expensive
sedan to swerve off the bridge and nose-
first into the green deep water to where it
was never found and he suspected if
he lived long enough he'd hear something
similar again. We all did.

## Reverend Paidoff

He sermonized each week, not
to the women, so much; he had them,
but to the men in the pews, who'd
managed the night before to be rolled
out of the deep and narrow mines,
their helmet beams bouncing,
announcing they'd won another day;
and in the cast-off bourbon barrels,
their wives soaked and scrubbed them.
Even so, they always had little black rims
around their soft dark lashes, their eyes
making them appear as lambs, as innocents,
but he knew them to be deceitful as
children, them with their thin shirts
buttoned up to hide their thick
red necks. And at the door, Reverend
couldn't help when he shook their hands
but notice the black lines in palms;
he felt sure God was showing him
the marks of Cain. Some's good people,
he supposed, or good enough. But them
others needed to be beat back with
the rod, so they don't never get the notion
they might rise from that mine before
they die, or that a bath oncet a week
up here on Earth, would ever be
enough to bring them clean.

## The Underman

Seems always I have axe
in hand and my muscles
burn from chopping.
I tote to warm
the house and strike
the match to set it all
going, then am told to move
away from the flame.

## Hoke Whiddle

He was supposed to be out hunting
with the boys, but he crouched instead
unseen at the edge of his woods and
watched Mr. Worldly come and go
every week. Hoke smoked filterless
Pall Malls, but coughed up a choke
only when the dust roared up from
Mr. Worldly's car thundering down
the lane. That reminds me that I meant
to say, too, and earlier on, that Hoke had
a shotgun in his lap and it felt hot
as an overburdened engine. It was a gun
I heard years later he regretted not
firing, though he knew he'd have to
have killed more than Worldly to set
his family right: there'd be his daughter
and her little one who'd need to be get rid
of too—and though he went with them,
he never loved hunting like his men
kin, was never fond of dragging what
he'd just shot out of the woods to be skinned
and butchered for the dinner table. So
he sat there each week, smoking,
trying to imagine how he'd feel
dragging something heavy
deep into Whiddle Wood.

## Edda Whiddle

When her mam told her
to walk the path between
their cabin and her daddy's
place, under the conifer
canopy, and after a good soft
spring mountain rain, now
and then she was lucky
to find bright yellow Indian
pipes sprouting up from
the moss found velvet under
her feet. They stood, in
her mind, like the crosses
of Golgotha, and reminded
her that any sin can be washed
clean, be forgiven. Even a sin
she had assumed from her mother.
When she saw those pipes,
she didn't want to come out
on the other far side into the
light, didn't want to leave
the dark woods' forgiveness, for it
seemed of no need then to go
asking him again for money.

## Derrick the Driver

I usually got me a few hours of time free.
I use them to keep the garage neat, oil off
the floor, all the leather wiped clean. Not
because I love a damned car, but because
I'm happy to have work and a place
to live over the garage. Sometimes, though,
when the morning is too lonely, I go up
and talk to Cook, or Bump Gardner,
who is lucky cause he owns his own
lawn service and has say in where, how,
and when he comes and goes. Then,
Mrs. Worldly has her gal call me and
I pull the car around front, wait for
the Old Mrs. to come down the steps,
fat Housekeeper at her elbow. Sometimes
we drive to Country Club and we're there
so long I can read a whole book. I like to read
Zane Grey, but McMurtry, too, about cowboys
and ranchers and about the days when a man
could start with nothing and end up rich.
The Worldlys had it all handed to them,
the distillery, the horses, the big house outside
the city. Silver spoon is what some say.
Sometimes she tells me to drive downtown.
She likes the blocks where the big department
stores used to be, likes to tell me about when
she was a girl, how she'd meet friends there
for tea—she sighs, she loves a high tea service,

she says, and I nod *yes, ma'am, I know you do*
and try not to smile, thinking of the times
she stirs and slurs, but she's pretty sure
I'm being smart, so I shut up and drive.
Around and around the same blocks, where
all the storefront windows stand empty,
*gray and dirty as mudflaps,* I say aloud.
*Just drive, Derrick, you get paid to drive.*

## Cook's Helper

Each time I press the cutter
into the soft white bread,
scalloped wheels pretty even
before I spread the smooth
green Benedictine, all for the ladies'
high tea, I think of my Mam,
across town, on the line, pulling
the hissing press, cutting steel
wheels from sheet metal,
both of us at work on
something uneatable.

## No Reference Coming

Today, Mrs. Worldly dismissed
the young parlor maid. She told
Derrick to wait with the car
out back, then drive the girl
away. *Where, Mrs.?* Derrick asked.
*Return her to her people, in South
City somewhere, how should I know
exactly where? But no farther,*
she slurred. Silly girl,
found where she oughtn't have
been caught so late at night.
I glanced up and seen Mrs.
at the bedroom window, her eyes
slit like a hawk's scanning
the field for a skinny mouse.
But when I hold the door
for Maid to go back down
the steps, I look up and see
Mrs. watching and she's changed
somehow, now an old crow,
rough and tatter-winged, slumped;
and it was maybe because she saw
that the young maid, changed into
her jeans, with her backpack thrown
over her shoulder, looked like
the young girl she is and not
anymore like the Mrs.'s Maid.

## Between Maid

I was hired by Mrs. Worldly
to be the between maid—to run
to the garage to tell the chauffeur
to bring round the car, to gather
dishes from the servant's table,
but other things, too, became my chores,
like the night Mister Billy Blueblood
tapped at my door, told me to follow him
up to his room where I went down
on the floor to scrub each spot of blood
from the wool carpet. He pointed there,
and there, and there. He pointed
as if each spot was a coin
he'd dropped and I should be happy
to pick up and put into my pocket.
In between, I knew not to say
anything, not a word about the parlor
maid, her toes I saw peeking out
from beneath the heavy velour curtains,
she shamed for having said nothing
to him when he called her up about
being in her monthlies. And that's
about all there is to say about how
I rose in this world, became Mrs.
Worldly's new parlor maid.

## The Working Poor

The working poor ain't allowed
no secrets but those of the Mrs.
and Mr. We ain't allowed no grief
neither. But worse we ain't even
supposed to show no sense of own
selves. If we dare wear something
pretty, even if it's cheap, they look
it over like we pulled it from
their own clothes heaped and set
aside for the charity truck. They see
us leaving out or coming in looking
good, they squint hard trying to
recollect if they'd ever have worn such
a skirt or could ever imagine pinning
a brooch like that to their thick furs.

## Phone Etiquette

I say *Have it all delivered*
*to Mrs. Worldly.*
She say *Is that W as in Wonder?*
I say, *No, W as in White*
*or add Wuh to a right.*
She say *O?*
I say *Yes, O,*
*as in Old money.*
*R,* she repeat.
*Yes, R you kidding?*
*R you predestined, chosen,*
*an old family of God?* She quiet
but then say *So you mean L as in*
*Light, Lamb, Love?*
*No.* I correct, and un-witness,
*L as in Long time ago*
*my family came to America*
*on the Mayflower.*
*O,* she say. *I see.*
*Not O, not C,* I say back. *D*
*as in Delightful, Delicious, Divine.*
*L,* she repeat.
*Yes, yes,* I sigh. *L-L-L-L that magic*
*Ladder by which all can pull themselves up*
*by their bootstraps—and a new shiny*
*Lincoln in the* gar-razhe.
*Y?* she say.
*Y?* I repeat. *Y that's just the way*

*it is, and Y is what we may always be*
*asking, till the Almighty Yanks us up*
*off this green earth to our delivered*
*reward up Yonder.*

## Elder Companion

She calls me names and swears
as if she still sits high and mighty,
and not covered in the foul sores
that my God requires I clean.

I don't know if she's in her right
mind or not. She can ring me
all she wants, for I'm free to leave
each day, freer than her, anyway.

# Advice to the Novice

*"Going alone with Tom? But why collect fresh fish
for all the old cats who can see you?"*

—E.P.

## Cupid

We two had long been friends, when after work
one night, my girlfriend and I sat at the bar.

She said "He's so adorable," and I said "Who?"
And she waggled her finger toward you, bent over

the pool table, long bangs in your eyes. Like so
many things then, I had to be told what I already

knew, before I could know it. You pulled back
the cue stick, the cue ball clacked soundly

against another. The red three spun hard across the table,
then rang the pocket before sinking wholeheartedly.

## Stranger at the Wedding

If the stranger drives up in a dark long car, turn away from
the window. Do not watch it roll up the graveled drive.

If the stranger wears a red shirt, tails untucked, then ask
your brother to greet him with caution.

If the stranger offers a gift, wrapped, and looking suspiciously
like a violin, wait until after the ceremony to open.

If, as he nears, the stranger becomes more familiar, continue
peeking from behind the lace curtain until sure he is not your ex-lover.

But if the stranger turns out to be a ghost from the groom's past—
the one murdered in own bed—invite her in while you finish

dressing. As your feet slip into white satin shoes, ask her to tell you
those things left unsaid. *Lie* to her. Tell her it is now or never.

## When to Congratulate a Bride

Never. Not even if you're thinking
holy mackerel, holy cannoli, not
even if you've gone on your knees
in Church and prayed for her—say
oh, finally *Lord!* and yes, God
is good! Not even if two-faced
you're really thinking *ha!* fat luck
she's got with that loser trash. All
that'd be like saying she'd done
something commendable to catch
him. Like she dove hard for a football
in the mud. Come up with it! Then
slid across the line in the last
three seconds of the game. It's best
to learn this right now and today.
What we see, we rarely ever say.

# Church of the Absent Mother

*after Charles Simic*

When opened, the glowing
sepulcher offers an endless font
of 2% milk, ever present
for the bowls of cold cereal.

The eye of the god is all
around. On the rangetop,
it seethes. In the laundry room,
it cries. The father at the door

comforts them as they run out
to school, as they re-enter
in the afternoon. He is generous,
too, with her, opening the door

wide, offering absolution
when he spies the taxi
in the drive. Returned home,
in the vestibule, her suitcase

slumps. In it are the bags
of t-shirts, hard foreign candies,
small weighted coins
that cannot purchase.

## Elocution Tutor

Don't *perform ablutions,* instead simply *wash.*
Don't go barge out of the *manor residence;*
simply leave your *house.* You are not *brainy*
for doing so, but you might be *brilliant,*
unless you say *goil* for *girl, eggsit* for
*exit,* and trill your *r* and hiss your *s* when
and if you ever do arrive in Par *ris* and
once there never say *I am forn,* never say
*I beg your pardon,* when you only mean
*excuse me,* especially if you have bumped into
a *Gempmum*—even if he is not a *Gentleman,*
which you will know if he rhymes *talk* with *bark,*
instead of *Bach* and shoves his grubby paws
into your *brazier,* instead of sliding his clean
manicured fingers into your *underwaist.*

## First Church

Later, they would accompany stolid women to the temple—
for they were only children and children are so often seduced
by the idea of Bible camp, the coloring books, the balloons,

the games with other children, the cookies frosted gaily
in the shapes of letters J,E,S,U,S. There the children's faces
were wiped, and their tongues came out to receive,

but all this came after and none of it, not the purple robes,
nor the white doves cut from paper and taped to the windows,
nor the great scenes of prophecy caught in lighted panes

could compare with the world's first sermon, the grand strange
bird seen, outstretched like a cross. It lay in the leaves
and pine needles, discovered at the wooded park,

and the children had dashed back through the leaves,
kicked through the leaves in their hurry to tell
and the aunt—the one with snakes tattooed

the length of her legs—she went with and down
and there it was, splayed, its underwings exposed
and speckled and dark like the inside of a shell

they'd discovered in the tide earlier that summer.
They hypothesized: the hail storm the night before

was something not withstood and had struck the bird
dead from its perch in the pine. They brought it offerings,

nubbins of fresh corn, strips from a T-Bone about to be lain
on the hot grill, dark wine in a paper cup. This was the first church

the children knew. Those other myths were not to be believed
because of what they had already seen, what they had been

able to learn without being told. Life was that up there
in the trees, the sky, the clouds, and death was what could be

found below, knocked cold down here to the earth. They knew this
because they had slipped their fingers through a yellow talon,

stiffened already into a round circle, a hollowed zero,
which always means more than nothing.

*In the Boqueria Market*


With my sixteen-year-old son, I walked through the heaps
of blushing mango and the skinned gray carcasses

of ducks and the clear wide eyes of red fish on ice on a table,
alongside rows of silvery sardines, the sprawling spiny

arms of crabs, the matte red shells of lobster, steamed and ready
to eat. My son seemed happier than in the Picasso Museum,

where earlier I had pointed out each of the blue paintings
I was so eager for him to see, wanting him to have this

and all the advantages his father and I could afford to give him.
In the Newark Airport, I had been giddy with the prospect

of it as we sat waiting to board our flight to Barcelona—
across the slick hall, another ticketed boy, but

in desert camouflage and heavy boots, backpack weighing
him down. The young soldier leaned against the wall,

and slid, collapsing, exhausted, to the floor. I wondered how far
he'd come already, from which small town his mother had

let him go, then, turned back to my own—until when at the market,
I looked up into the coarse rafters, where with gay yellow

flowers and fragrant bouquets of herbs, in the air lambs hung
and slowly revolved. An old merchant touched my arm

and quickly changed his tongue from Catalan to rough English. He
pointed up and said, *Yes! Yes! Fresh lamb very good for your supper.*

## Head Come Off

So we think for we cannot
not think his head come off
without we feel our heads
coming off or our children's
heads or our lovers' heads
or our mother's heads
we think our heads off
then we think their heads
must come off in our heads
we would carry their heads
in bowling ball bags
and unzip to show all
the kids at the bus stop because
well because his head come off
and our heads still on.

## Prom Goers

The girls come out in spring like young vegetables
emerging from a garden. Their dresses clingy and smooth
at their hips; they are yellow squash blossoms; or,
in their one-shouldered straps, tendrils of sweet peas twining up
tanned athletic trellises. One girl in white, her blond hair atop
her head, is a strawberry bud; another—mine—
is as feathery as new dill shooting from its stalk. Some
of the boys have heads like winter cabbages, benign.
But, others are small furry animals. They try to hide
it from the photograph, but I won't need to look at it later. I see
now in their eyes how ready they are to take their first sharp bite.

## Restoration and Repair

When walking under the blue flapping tarp
that covers the hole where the arching stained
glass window of the great gray craggy cathedral

on Sixth Street has been removed to be scrubbed
and repaired, imagine the apostles as they might now be,
as they lay un-banded, un-hooked from their bindings,

their chains and belts, their heavy lead boundaries.
Imagine them numbered and systematized, as if
they may be studied rationally. See them as they lay

in pieces like boats of loose glass floating across
the great wooden tables of B & C Stained Restoration
and Repair. There the glass artist lifts a leering eye,

now unmoored from some saint. The artist holds it
between her fingers, sees that it floats eerily
within a milky sphere as if in a fishbowl.

Does she know she is the new maker? And that it's all
up to her to re-gather these tired old men, up to her
to send them on a different dusty journey or set them

asail unknown for centuries asea. Will she feel
the command now to rescue the spirit of the body
from the rope? Will she know what to do with that

evil eye or the irregular shard, deconstructed and now more
fully examined, revealing neatly manicured fingertips.
Restorer, un-pry the fingers of the gouty old saint who clutches

too tightly the shoulder of a small boy. Gather the yellow
glass from each stiff halo. Maker, it is time to give us
another version of light shining from some newly made sun.

## The Fruit Knife

In my hand, the fruit knife seems smaller,
but razor-sharp, its handle, bone, unlike
the other silver service, signifies its own
strange work. I asked for it to be set
this morning because the table holds a footed bowl
of freckled pear and Honeycrisp.
Last night, Mr. Worldly passed by my door,
again, his footsteps steady as an iambic line.
Not that long ago, you know, I could lie in bed,
hear his shoes stop, caesura-like, outside
my room. Now there is only measured passing.
Dear, to use this knife properly, plunge it—
watch—into rolling heart of the Anjou. Take care
it does not divide unevenly, leaving one side small,
all flesh; and the other with full core of seed, memory
of silver branch, where the fruit dangled deliciously
if only for a short debutante season. Do not act timidly or
you will knick your own hands, leaving those cuts,
small, but deep enough for salt to easily settle.

## Details of Interest to the Hostess

In the dark pantry, two highball glasses, one
empty, the other a melting amber mess, rim
waxy with articulated pink lips, an ashtray,
a cliché, still smoldering, cigarette interrupted,
a space now quickly collapsing in on itself
like sand at the edge of an empty unmarked grave.
Upon the counter, ah! she finds what she's been
searching for, a single peculiar thread, and now
her eyes hunt for more, a hair from a head,
a missing button. She examines the bowl of shiny
green apples, vibrant, quivering, all seem to be
mouth-wateringly unbitten, unnibbled, but she knows
better, and turns each, looking for slight tooth marks.

## Oyster Fork

It is as it should be. Useful.
Like a reputable sturdy
farmyard tool, and not
the ridiculously pitched fork
of the devil or a water-logged
god. It suits what I'm after,
which isn't the fine pearl—
nor am I after the hesitant
comma of a pink prawn,
its fin left to putter
like the rotor
of a motor on a boat
slowly pulling its captain out
to the middle of
a desolate gray lake;
nor do I care
for the shy clam;
nor am I fooled by the mica
of the mussel shell,
forever promising to open
itself like a woman.
What I'm after
is the slippery fish
just arranged on its lettuce
bed, its fleshy beckoning,
an honest presentation—
for once—
of what it is
and what it wants.

## Spoon

If I were
a silver
spoon,
I'd bite
my own
lip, stay
wordless,
whimper
lightly,
as your
initials
were ta-
tooed on
the stem
of my
chased
blossom.
I would offer
my slick tongue for
your sticky amber honey.
Having been pulled and pulled
around and around through your
steamy tea, I'd swoon, lie back
happily, pooled, filled with
your hot, sweet,
cajolery.

## Get Back to Sleep

In my dream, I was
but a girl,
a debutante
in a full white skirt.
I waved and shouted
from a high window.
Flames flew out
in curtains that caught wind.
A man, my father,
a fine figure,
and his two sons,
my brothers,
stand under the steady health
of a wide hickory tree.
They threw words
up into the air like water
from full buckets:
*jump! jump!* The words
were vaulted
into the air until
they broke apart
into letters,
the *j* falls,
then the *u* and the *m*
and the *p*.
All into the out-
stretched apron of Cook
below. *Jump*, Cook cried,
again. I yelped:

*I'm afraid. I'm*
*afraid. I know you won't*
*catch me.* Then the hem
of my white
gauzy skirt caught fire
and just before
I woke, I had been
watching the flame gain.

## First High Tea Service

I remember the hands of my guests,
gloved, ducked, and darted like blind
albino fish. Their shared goal: to avoid
all light. I rang: Cook waddled in
with the tray, the silver-chased teapot,
just inherited, proud and full
of boiling water. I poured it steadily
into the hand-painted rosebuds
rimming around each white cup.
Steam rose as if the ghost
of young Franklin, killed
in that ridiculous foreign war.
He seemed to be kicking
his feet through the thick air
of that room, trying to swim up
to heaven. If I'd married him, my
mother would have kept me in all-black
for a year. There were little sausages,
thin round sandwiches to dip in
mayonnaise, sweets with peaked nipples.
The women tugged at their fingertips,
stripping down daintily as if they were in
the presence of their husbands.
They dropped sugar cubes into
the bright Earl Grey, stirred them
into nothing. They tipped, sipped,
and smiled, knowing each of them,
easily, but at first opportunity,

would turn any other into cold
gray stone, like stalagmites hanging
from the ceiling of Mammoth Cave,
when Franklin and I had visited
two summers before, where I'd said
to him *they look like sleeping bats*
and he had laughed and told me
I was very *very* clever.

## Neat Penmanship for the Lady

It is said *a neat, precise,*
*evenly written note*
*portrays a person*
*of those characteristics,*
so when writing
your betraying husband,
feminize your furious
cursive—don't risk
blurred black ink
and blot. Don't let
your letters dash on
without you,
as if fanned by
great bellows. Nor
should you allow
your margins to rise
up in a storm
of gnashing black waves,
appearing as if
they might be able
to thrash a great ship.
Rather carry
the weight of those words,
and bring the burden
down with trembling
hand and heart to pound
the waxy seal. After
all, you made a promise
to him; when you signed

your name, you gave
your implicit word
that you would keep
private all sloppy spills.

## A House Put Back to Order

Afterward, this house
cannot simply be
swept up, dusted,
laundered, and remade
with hospital corners,
ship-shape. The words
were said. You heard
the filthy syllables.

And so, how does one
begin to tidy this?
The half left behind
subsequent to the sudden
snap, that crack moving
through ice, the ice
calving apart in a part
nearly equal to the berg.

You stand in your half
of the house watching
the other—the bathtub,
but not the sink, the
dresser, but not
the bed, like blue
ice, floating away.

# In a Time of Bereavement

*Everything is done to avoid unnecessary evidence
of the change that has taken place.*

—E.P.

## What the Girl Wore

At the store, on the hanger, the blue dress must have fallen
like water to a froth of frilled hem, its bodice as smocked
as a christening gown. A season out of date, her mother chose it
from our local department store chiefly for the high collar,
but I knew it was a dress Lisa wouldn't have been caught
dead in. Just hidden under the neckband of lace, the circle
of her purple necklace, each dark bead a fingertip of efficient
bruise that we already knew about anyway, and simply went on
imagining, as we, her classmates, filed past the white coffin.

*Undertaking*

I wonder about those
who dress the dead,
after the body has been
bathed, after the body
has grown stiffer
with abandonment.
It must be like
putting clothes on a doll
that is loved, but
also loathed
for never quite rising
to fulfill its lie
of the life-like.

I wonder about those
who powder the noses
and rouge the lips
of the dead. The one whose
hand pulled Lisa's hair
through the brush,
the one who decided not
to braid her hair
into one long swish,
as we'd most often seen
on the sandy ball field,

but had decided instead
to twist it up atop her head
into a formal knot. Unkind
unknown, you, who
obliged us to see
Lisa as the woman
she would never be.

## Young Angel of Darkness

My pet grandfather had not been told
by doctors or nurses, nor my grandmother

that what he had was lung cancer and that
that cancer was quickly killing him. It was common then

to keep this sort of secret from the dying, and at twelve,
I'd be dumb to it, too, but I'd heard them discussing

an exception for me, not yet old enough to visit
that sick ward. Riding up the elevator, I felt the burden

bear down on me, my mother's slim hand gently squeezed
my shoulder: *Remember now, let's not talk about anything*

*sad. Try to cheer him up, okay? Smile.* When the elevator doors
opened, the buoyancy of the white humming lights lifted me

like water. I floated down the hall and into his room as if
I were a small boat drifting to beach. The air, gauzy

and thick, contrasted with the starchy hospital sheets.
I glided over to my grandfather and for the first time

saw fear in his eyes; and then love, then again,
fear. I knew I must not say the truth out loud,

but just then I grew heady and arrogant
with my grown-up secret. I could not contain it.

I extended my hand. *Come with me*, I beckoned
wordlessly, seductively, and he took my hand.

I squeezed hard. With my eyes, I said, *Don't let go.*
*And don't tell. I won't,* he blinked. *Then, hold on*

*tight,* I demanded with my narrowing eyes: *I'm going*
*to lead you down the dark tunnel of truth.*

## Where Had It Gone?

Where had it gone? My bravery for
      tenderness?
Inside a square stone fence,
      there, a horse, there, then,
      (though then I had not recognized it),
a mare, nodding, nodding,
to me—
      her head, she shook, she
walked over bashfully, one hoof lightly bent
inches above
before it met grass—
      she said,
      I remember *you,*

large steady eyes rolling up coquettishly.
      My hands opened, both lay open and empty
on top of the rough stone fence.
She placed her muzzle
      into one pink palm—
      she placed her muzzle into the other,
her nose supple and pink—
      I turning wholly pink—

her strong teeth slightly revealed
      and a quiver of delight
began to undulate through her body.
      From mane through bony ridge
of mountainous back, over her back,
      a ridge of trim mountain,

quiver running down like
sound moving,
      and then settling
in her muscled and dappled
flank until it flipped out
      of her tail,

      I scratch the gray star
on her face, look into her eyes,
brave, gentle girl. Dark
benevolence I find here.

## In a Diner Somewhere in Iowa, I Imagine My Father Meeting the Future President

He would have been sitting at the counter, waiting
for a greasy truck part to arrive from Davenport
when Nixon walked into the joint.

He would have been more attentive to
the slim black-haired waitress with the coffee pot
than the politician's entourage,

but when she turned to take another's order,
he would have noticed the dark gray wool suit
Nixon wore through the Midwestern heat of August

and the way Nixon awkwardly flirted with the folks
in the booths lining the window, mainly old women
who barely looked up from dunking their dry toast into tea.

My father would have shaken the hand of Nixon
who made his way one by one down
the working class men on stools at the counter,

but my father would have said later
that Nixon's hands were damp and pink,
soft like some rich girl's.

And when my father returned home
to my mother the next week, after
unloading La-Z-Boy recliners and boxes of record albums

and banana-seat bikes, he would have said
to her *If that's the best we can do,*
*we got a whole world of trouble.*

But there would have been a change in my father
after Nixon won the White House.
My father would have become interested in things

he'd never questioned before. While driving his rig
cross country, he would have killed boredom by
holding imagined conversations with Nixon,

telling what Nixon ought to do to ease the plight
of the working man. At first, it would be funny
when my father'd say at dinner: *You know what I told Dick*

*when I was going through Oklahoma? I said, Dick,*
*I ain't like you, Dick. I didn't get to college. I never had things*
*handed to me. I got one suit and it's for funerals.* He'd shake

his fork at the TV and joke, *I told my man there*
*the only China I care about is what them*
*housewives unwrap, me watching*

*and waiting for all hell to break loose when they find*
*a cracked tea cup.* My father's conversations would grow
darker with each year of Nixon's administration.

*You should have got them out, Dick, goddammit,* he'd swear,
slowing behind the funeral processions
along some state highway, driving past, looking

in his rearview at the old men, hats on their hearts,
standing next to their cars parked on the shoulder
of the road. Then, with wrecked grief, *get them out now.*

He'd have explained how he'd have been there
too, but got turned back because when a boy
his heart was torn apart by rheumatic fever.

That night, when at home, watching Nixon resign,
for once he would have been happy
(or at least happier), seen a larger world view

and understood something complicated
was trying to be put right, instead of
crying and agitating his ill-treated heart, and

blaming himself for the rest of his life that it was his kid
brother, on his second tour, who was killed in the bush
of Vietnam. Or at least that's what I can imagine.

## War Hits Home

Boswell the Butler
adjusted the black wreath
on the front door, noting
to himself that around back,
at the service entrance, there
could have hung three more.

## Elegy for the Busboy

These years later, I still remember
how much I loved working with you,
how I always gladly gave you more
than your 10%, because
you never grumbled or groused,
seemed to carry so effortlessly
those trays: dirty plates stacked ten
or twelve high, empty wine bottles
poised and tall, green luminous glass
perfectly balanced as you made your way
coolly composed from the front of the house
into the hellish heart of the small

noisy kitchen, but restaurant folks
always seem to have some other lives
they are waiting to live. We heard about yours
at the beginning of our Thursday night shift
because Joe, our standby bartender, also
moonlighted as a coroner's photographer
while hoping his own pictures would go up
in some hot gallery on Market.

Joe leaned against the silver stainless
counter, telling all he knew to the prep cooks
readying their *mise en place*: the salad girl
slicing white coins from the hearts of palm,
the sous chef's knife knocking quickly
against the wooden board. I heard Joe say
*bedroom, shotgun.* Within that hum, it took

a moment to realize the dishwasher, who spoke
no English, was motioning he needed by.
He carried a high clean stack of plates,
a dozen. They leaned precariously within
his extended arms like a small Tower
of Pisa. Frail, overburdened Atlas.
I never did learn what faraway country
he'd left to come to America.

*Page 278, Always at a Distance from the Door*


In my blue

*Etiquette*, she tells me had I decided
to bring you home

I should have taken care to place
your casket "in the drawing room,"

in front of the mantel, or
between two windows—
but always at a distance

from the front door, for don't mourners always need
 a moment more

to wipe their feet before walking in to
pay respects to the departed?

It's as if I'm reading how to arrange
fruit, pears and apples, ripening
in a porcelain bowl.

But, where to place you,
found three? four? days after, so alone,

already beginning to mummify,
the coroner said, when I drove up
to sign the papers. On his desk,
a worn municipal file:

inside an official report,
and a penciled drawing, illustrating
how you were found,
outstretched on the floor, blocking

the front door. In a plastic bag,
one set of keys "discovered
next to," documented in the sketch
by a little yellow circle.

Each time I see it I try to imagine
something else,
a small sun, an ochre
blossom, a mum,

a wedding ring out of plumb.

Anything but those keys
as keys, a jangling clutch lost

for twenty years, and now found.
Keys useless to open
any door,
useless to open anything more.

## Page 273, Hanging the Bell

In my blue
     *Etiquette*, she tells me
after your death,

I should have gathered purple flowers
and streamed a black ribbon

from the bell on my door.
     Purple, black
     because *you* weren't

a child. A child

would have demanded white
streamers, white
flowers.

     But *I am* your child.

     And isn't *what* I was
     also *now* departed?

## Blue Etiquette

We had gone to visit her
Indiana folks, my grandmother
and I, to leave a pot of autumn
flowers, to pinch a weed or two,
and on driving out, pulled over
to see the girl's gravesite, her
marker, a dollhouse, taller than
me not yet in school. I peered
through rippled glass windows,
fogging the little panes with
my uneven breath. Upstairs,
bedrooms with scalloped
canopies and floral fringed
rugs, in one, a chest, opened
to tiny folded linens; then,
as if having just been called,
my eyes traveled down
the staircase, skipping steps as if
I were running. My gaze turned
right into the dining room,
a delicate lace tablecloth,
over carved legs that ended
in fierce animal feet—
and, tiny dime-sized china
plates, petite blue rosettes
painted around their rims. Looking
in, just then, I saw the place
that had been set for me.

## Lament

*for Claudia Emerson*

After a night of drinking moon-
shine, after our husbands
walked away, shaking
their heads, once, long ago, we swung

in a porch swing chained between two
sycamores. We pumped our
feet and swung, trying to
sing "Wild Nights! Wild Nights!" to the tune

of "The Yellow Rose of Texas."
The swing dipped and rose, rose
and dipped so riotously
high that a hitch entered our song, turning

all air anapestic, that final
extra hitch unchaining
the swing. Hurtling through
unbowered space, we hung for a

moment like astronauts, our dark
shadows against the full
bright moon, and we knew when
we fell back to the hard earth, there

was a good chance one or both of
us would be gravely hurt,
but seconds later, we lay
sprawled across the night-wetted grass

of Southern Virginia, and
looking up, up into
the patient sky, we laughed
and laughed, realizing, at least in

that moment, we weren't hurt.
Not in that moment, we weren't.

## Her Mother's Marriages
## Drift like Boats in Her Mind

1

The first is a slight canoe, teaked
and slim, scoring through
the mystery of dark pond
water, lit with wet bone.

Arrogant bow, chin
up, it believes a sudden downpour
is the meanest storm
it will be called to endure.

2 & 3

Within the sturdy houseboat, the
curtains are trimmed
with blue fringe that sways
as the hulk rocks

in the wake of

a speedboat careening by.
It's a Chris-Craft, new, red-bellied,
the waterline circling low.
The driver turns again, goes

by once more. He waves. At night,
the houseboat squats near shore, lightly
rocking in shallow waters,

all windows dark, except one
small lighted circle.

3

If awake, one could hear
the low growl of a speedboat
on the lake at night, then
the motor cut. One could see
the window go dark.

3 & 4

The last is a trawler, awkward
but steady, dependable,
like the lumbering
boats sent out after
the body has risen
to the surface. She who

has leapt from the top

of the falls, believes
even as plunging toward
the rock and violent
eddies of the Niagara River

that the barrel will keep
her safe as a boat.

*Coda*

And some were taken
to shore by the wake,
while others drifted toward
the dark heart of the lake.

# Notes & Shorter Letters

Emily Post's 1922 edition of *Etiquette* is the source of many subjects, titles, or epigraphs in this collection, including "Have Silver That Shines or None," "Interviewing the Applicant," "Stranger at the Wedding," "When to Congratulate the Bride," "Elocution Tutor," "Details of Interest to the Hostess," "Neat Penmanship for the Lady," "A House Put Back to Order," "Page 273, Hanging the Bell," and "Page 278, Always at a Distance from the Door."

Likewise many of the names of characters in poems are taken from *Etiquette* as well, including Mrs. Worldly, Mr. Worldly, the Oldlineages, the Gildings, and the Wellborns, though others are of my own imagination.

## Biographical Note

Kathleen Driskell is the author of three previous collections of poetry, *Laughing Sickness* (Fleur-de-Lis Press), *Seed Across Snow* (Red Hen Press), listed as a national bestseller by the Poetry Foundation, and *Next Door to the Dead*, a Kentucky Voices Selection of the University Press of Kentucky. She also published *Peck and Pock: A Graphic Poem*, a long illustrated poem in comic book form. Her poems have appeared in *The Southern Review*, *The North American Review*, *The Greensboro Review*, *River Styx*, *Shenandoah*, *Appalachian Heritage*, *Plume*, and other literary journals, as well as online at *American Life in Poetry*, *Poetry Daily*, and *Verse Daily*. She is an Al Smith Fellow of the Kentucky Arts Council and serves as the Associate Program Director of Spalding University's low-residency Master of Fine Arts Program in Louisville, Kentucky, where she lives with her family in an old church built before the American Civil War.

CPSIA information can be obtained at www.ICGtesting.com
Printed in the USA
BVOW08s2352260916

R7458100001B/R74581PG462452BVX1B/1/P